Introduction to 🌐 EARTH'S RESOURCES

HOW WE USE
ROCKS AND MINERALS

Ruth Daly

Crabtree Publishing Company
www.crabtreebooks.com

Crabtree Publishing Company
www.crabtreebooks.com

Author: Ruth Daly
Editorial Director: Kathy Middleton
Editor: Ellen Rodger
Picture Manager: Sophie Mortimer
Design Manager: Keith Davis
Children's Publisher: Anne O'Daly
Proofreader: Debbie Greenberg
**Production coordinator and
  Prepress technician:** Ken Wright
Print coordinator: Katherine Berti

Library and Achives Canada Cataloguing in Publication

Title: How we use rocks and minerals / Ruth Daly.
Names: Daly, Ruth, 1962- author.
Description: Series statement: Introduction to Earth's resources | Includes bibliographical references and index.
Identifiers: Canadiana (print) 20200284045 | Canadiana (ebook) 20200284088 | ISBN 9780778781899 (softcover) | ISBN 9780778781837 (hardcover) | ISBN 9781427126016 (HTML)
Subjects: LCSH: Rocks—Juvenile literature. | LCSH: Minerals—Juvenile literature.
Classification: LCC QE432.2 .D35 2020 | DDC j552—dc23

Library of Congress Cataloging-in-Publication Data

Names: Daly, Ruth, author.
Title: How we use rocks and minerals / Ruth Daly.
Description: New York : Crabtree Publishing Company, 2021. | Series: Introduction to earth's resources | Includes index.
Identifiers: LCCN 2020029719 (print) | LCCN 2020029720 (ebook) | ISBN 9780778781837 (hardcover) | ISBN 9780778781899 (paperback) | ISBN 9781427126016 (ebook)
Subjects: LCSH: Rocks--Juvenile literature. | Minerals--Juvenile literature.
Classification: LCC QE432.2 .D35 2021 (print) | LCC QE432.2 (ebook) | DDC 553--dc23
LC record available at https://lccn.loc.gov/2020029719
LC ebook record available at https://lccn.loc.gov/2020029720

Crabtree Publishing Company
www.crabtreebooks.com   1-800-387-7650
Published in 2021 by Crabtree Publishing Company

Copyright © Brown Bear Books Ltd 2020

Published in Canada
Crabtree Publishing
616 Welland Ave.
St. Catharines, ON
L2M 5V6

Published in the United States
Crabtree Publishing
347 Fifth Ave
Suite 1402-145
New York, NY 10016

Printed in the U.S.A./082020/CG20200710

In Canada: We acknowledge the financial support of the Government of Canada through the Canada Book Fund for our publishing activities.

Contents

What Are Rocks and Minerals?

Rocks and minerals are everywhere on Earth. They are on mountain peaks, deep underground, and under the ocean.

Rocks can be as small as pebbles or as large as a cliff. They come in many colors. Some rocks are hard. Other rocks are soft and break easily. Scientists put rocks into three main groups. These groups are igneous rocks, metamorphic rocks, and sedimentary rocks. All rocks are made up of minerals.

The hardest mineral is diamond. It is used in jewelry, to cut glass, and in drills.

The oldest rocks on Earth formed 4 billion years ago.

The Grand Canyon in Arizona is made of rock.

Minerals

Different amounts and types of minerals make up different types of rocks. Minerals are made of chemical **elements**, such as oxygen or **silicon**. Some minerals contain metals, such as iron. Minerals that contain metals are called **ores**. Most minerals have a mixture of elements. Some only contain one.

There are 4,000 different kinds of minerals on Earth.

Why Are Rocks and Minerals Important?

Most of our planet is made of rocks and minerals. We use them every day and in many different ways.

Humans have been using rocks and minerals since ancient times. People who lived in the **Stone Age** made tools from rocks. Rocks have also long been used to make shelters and buildings. Today, we use minerals in computers, cars, toys, and many other things.

Long ago, people used hard rocks such as flint to make arrowheads.

Humans started using stone tools and weapons about **2.6 million** years ago.

Bats hang upside down as they sleep and rest in caves during the daytime.

Rocks and Nature

Rocks are important in nature too. Caves, which are hollowed-out rock, provide shelter for many animals. Bats sleep in caves during the day. Brown bears hibernate there in the winter. Seabirds make nests in the cracks of cliffs. Minerals in the soil are also important in nature. They provide **nutrients** that help plants grow.

Each summer, 15 million Mexican free-tailed bats roost in Bracken Cave, Texas.

The Rock Cycle

Rocks take millions of years to form. They are always changing from one kind of rock to another. This is called the rock cycle.

Earth has different layers, like an onion. The outer layer is called the crust. This is the thinnest layer. It is hard and made of solid rock. The next layer is called the mantle. This layer is made of hot, melted rock called **magma**. At the center of Earth is the core. This part is mainly iron. The outer core is liquid but the inner core is solid.

Earth

Earth has three main zones: the crust, the mantle, and the core.

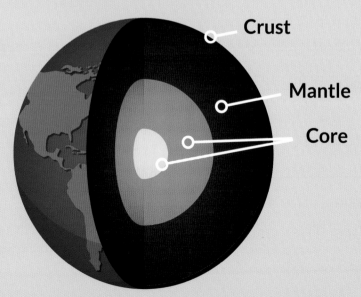

- Crust
- Mantle
- Core

Earth's crust is only **3 to 5 miles** (4.8 to 8 km) thick under the oceans.

How Rocks Are Made

Sedimentary rocks are made near Earth's surface. They form when small pieces of rock, called sediments, are pressed together. Igneous rocks form from molten magma that has cooled down. Metamorphic rocks are made when igneous rocks or sedimentary rocks are squeezed together and heated inside Earth.

The crust is up to **30 miles** (50 km) thick under mountain ranges.

The force of the wind has worn away the middle of this rock.

How Do We Use Rocks and Minerals?

How often do you nibble on chocolate, draw with a pencil, or brush your teeth?

All of these activities use rocks and minerals! We use rocks and minerals every day. People make buildings out of stone. We travel in cars, buses, and trains made from iron. We drink from cans made from aluminum. Minerals called rare earth metals are used in electronics and smartphones.

A smartphone contains about 75 chemical elements. All of these come from minerals.

Most smartphones use around **60** different metals to make them work.

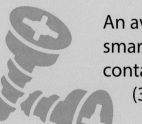

An average smartphone contains **1.1 oz** (33 g) of iron.

Rocks and minerals are used to make roads, as well as the cars and trucks that travel on them.

Minerals Keep Us Healthy!

Our bodies need minerals to grow and stay healthy. Calcium helps build strong bones. Iron carries oxygen around our bodies. Zinc helps our bodies fight disease. We get these minerals from our food. Calcium comes from dairy foods, such as milk, cheese, and yogurt. Meat, cheese, and eggs are rich in iron. We get zinc from nuts and beans.

Mining Rocks and Minerals

Rocks and minerals are found in the ground. How do we get them out?

Rocks and minerals are dug out of the ground from deep pits, called quarries, and **mines**. Quarries have been used for thousands of years. In ancient times, people cut stone by hand. They used tools such as hammers and picks. Today, huge machines dig out the rock. Sometimes explosives are used to blast the rock loose.

The stone circle at Stonehenge in England was built 5,000 years ago.

Ancient people dug the massive stones by hand.

The largest stones each weigh **25 tons** (23 metric tons).

They were moved **18.6 miles** (30 km) from the quarry where they were dug.

Deeper and Deeper

Some rocks are close to Earth's surface. People dig the ores containing iron or aluminum in big open mines. Other minerals are buried deep underground. Miners dig long tunnels, or shafts, into the earth. They **extract** the ores with machines and drills or blast it with explosives. The ores are taken back to the surface. Some of the deepest mines are gold mines.

In open mines, people strip away rocks and soil to get to the ores.

Clean Rocks and Minerals

Minerals are often joined to other elements. We have to remove the other materials to get the useful minerals.

Some minerals are almost pure when they come out of the ground. Most minerals are mixed with other substances and have to be **processed** to be separated. Many metals are removed from their ores by a process called smelting. In smelting, the ore is heated and chemicals are added.

Iron is the main metal that is smelted. The smelting takes place in a very hot blast furnace.

Smelting iron began more than **3,500** years ago.

The temperature in a blast furnace can go up to **3,000 ºF** (1,650 ºC).

Granite is cut out into slabs and polished before being made into countertops.

From Quarry to Kitchen

Granite is an igneous rock. It is tough and lasts for a long time. It is used for kitchen countertops, floor tiles, and paving stones. Granite is mined from quarries. Powerful machines and explosives dig it out in blocks. The granite is cut, smoothed, and polished before being cut into shapes ready to be used in our homes.

Rocks and Minerals Around the World

Some countries have more rocks and minerals than others. They sell the resources to countries that need them.

Coal is a sedimentary rock that is burned as fuel. China mines most of the world's coal. China is also the biggest producer of gold, although South Africa and Australia have more gold reserves, or stocks.

In 1848 gold was found in California. People from all over the world went there to make their fortune.

Between 1848 and 1855, more than **300,000** people came to look for gold.

Two miners dug **$17,000** worth of gold in one week.

Early gold miners washed stones in a pan to look for loose gold pieces.

A miner drills into rock to make holes for explosives.

Metal Mines

China also produces 90 percent of the world's rare earth metals. These metals are found in small amounts in Earth's crust all over the world. Only certain places have a big enough supply to mine. Other useful metals are iron and aluminum. Iron is mined in South Africa, the United States, and China. Bauxite is the ore that contains aluminum. It is mined in Australia, India, and Brazil.

Too Many Rocks and Minerals

In some parts of the world, rocks and minerals can cause natural disasters.

Earth's crust is made of huge plates. These plates fit together like pieces of a jigsaw puzzle. **Volcanoes** form in some of the places where these plates meet. When a volcano erupts, hot ash and gases are thrown into the air. Hot, molten **lava** flows from the volcano.

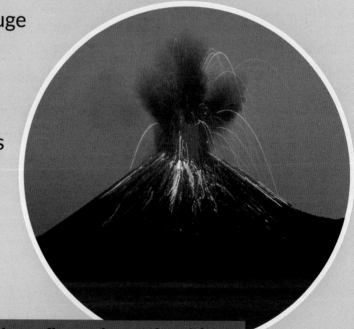

Lava flows down the sides of a volcano and destroys everything in its path.

The lava that comes out of a volcano can be 2,282 ⁰F (1,250 ⁰C)!

Landslides

A **landslide** happens when rocks and soil slip from the ground underneath them. The rocks slide down a slope. Landslides can be caused by heavy rain. The water makes the soil heavier than usual. Human activities, such as cutting down forests, can make landslides more likely to happen.

Landslides travel at **10–25 miles per hour** (16–40 km/h)!

Landslides cause a lot of damage. They may even destroy whole towns.

Rocks, Minerals, and Energy

Some minerals are used to produce energy. We use them for electricity and to heat our homes.

Coal is a **fossil fuel**. It was made from plants that lived millions of years ago. Coal is a **non-renewable** fuel, which means we will eventually run out of it. It is also harmful when it is burned. Coal **pollutes** the air and adds to gases that are heating the planet. We need less harmful ways to make **energy**.

Minerals are used to make solar panels and wind turbines.

Coal produces about **40%** of the world's electricity.

Uranium ore is found in small amounts in rocks.

Clean Energy

Uranium is a metal. It is used to make nuclear energy. This is also a type of energy that is non-renewable. However, nuclear energy makes less pollution than coal. Renewable energy is a better choice. Resources such as the Sun and wind will never run out. Renewable energy relies on using minerals. They are found in solar panels and wind **turbines**.

2.2 lbs (1 kg) of uranium creates as much energy as **1,500 tons** (1,360 metric tons) of coal.

Pollution

Minerals are useful, but some can be harmful, too. Mining rocks and minerals can also cause pollution.

Lead is a metal that has been used for thousands of years. In Ancient Rome, lead was used to make water pipes. More recently, it was used in paint and gasoline. We now know that lead is harmful to health, especially for young children. It is still used in car batteries, but many other uses have been banned.

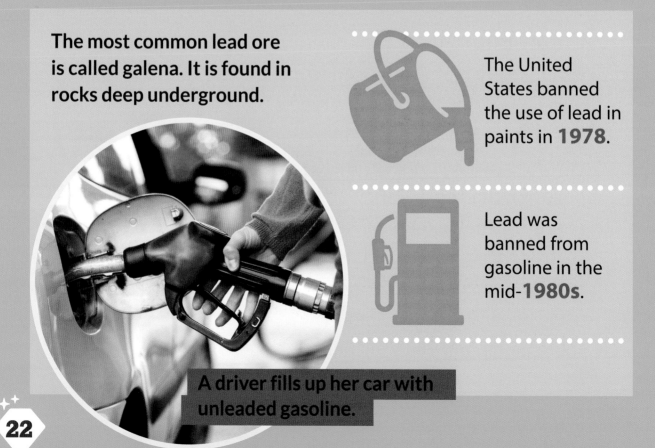

The most common lead ore is called galena. It is found in rocks deep underground.

The United States banned the use of lead in paints in **1978**.

Lead was banned from gasoline in the mid-**1980s**.

A driver fills up her car with unleaded gasoline.

Chemicals from a copper mine have polluted the water in this river.

Bad for the Environment

Mining creates waste and harms the **environment**. Sometimes chemicals used in the mining process leak. This can pollute drinking water and poison farmland. Landscapes are destroyed in open pit mining. Trees and plants are removed, which means that wildlife habitats are destroyed, too.

Rocks and Minerals for Fun

Rocks and minerals have serious uses, but we can enjoy them in fun ways, too!

Some people enjoy rock climbing. They climb rocks to reach the top. Bouldering is another type of rock climbing. People climb without a rope on small cliffs and boulders. While some people like to climb, others enjoy going deep into Earth! Potholers explore caves deep underground.

The Imperial State Crown is one of the Crown Jewels of the United Kingdom.

The crown has **2,868** diamonds.

It also has **269** pearls, **17** sapphires, **11** emeralds, and **4** rubies.

The crown is worn by the British queen or king on special occasions.

Precious Minerals

Many precious and valuable items are made from minerals. Gold and silver are used to make jewelry and coins. Precious stones that have been cut and polished are called gemstones. Rubies and sapphires are different forms of a mineral called corundum. Other gemstones are opals and emeralds.

Potholers wear special clothes to protect them as they explore caves.

Saving Rocks and Minerals

Even though rocks and minerals are all around us, it is important not to waste them.

Rocks and minerals are valuable resources. They are non-renewable. If we use them all up, there won't be any more. We need to **conserve** them. Reducing, reusing, and recycling products made from rocks and minerals will help us use less of these resources.

It takes less energy to make products from recycled metals than from materials from the ground.

100 million steel cans are used in the United States every day.

Making aluminum from recycled metal uses **95%** less energy than using materials from the ground.

26

The Eden Project in England was built on land from an old quarry.

New from Old

Stone from old buildings that is still in good condition can be reused in new buildings. The old buildings are carefully taken apart so that material can be used again. Steel is used to make cans for soup, fruit, and other foods. The steel comes from iron. The cans can be collected and recycled. Recycling steel cans keeps them out of a **landfill**. It prevents pollution by reducing the need for mining.

What Can I Do?

Rocks and minerals are important resources. Here are some ways you can save them.

- Rare earth metals are used in electronic devices. Protect your laptops, smartphones, and tablets so they don't get broken.

- Batteries contain cobalt, nickel, manganese, and aluminum. Find out if any local stores recycle batteries.

- Don't throw drink or food cans in the trash! Recycle steel cans and aluminum cans and encourage your family to do the same.

- Get creative! With help from an adult, turn clean metal food cans into holders for pens and pencils, candle holders, and pots for plants.

Quiz

How much have you learned about rocks and minerals? It's time to test your knowledge!

1. What are rocks made of?

a. grains
b. minerals
c. seeds

2. Where are rocks and minerals found?

a. Earth's core
b. Earth's crust
c. bread crust

3. What is the rock cycle?

a. the process of how rocks change over time
b. the process of making rocking chairs
c. the process of how rocks are mined

4. What can cause landslides?

a. too much rain making the land unstable
b. too many flowers growing on the land
c. not enough rain in the summer

5. Where is uranium found?

a. on the planet Uranus
b. in rocks in Earth
c. in paint and gasoline

Answers on page 32.

Glossary

conserve To protect something and not use it up

elements Substances that cannot be broken down into other substances

energy Power to make something work

environment The living and non-living surroundings on Earth

extract To remove or take something out

fossil fuel A fuel made from the remains of living things that died millions of years ago

landfill A place where waste materials are buried; a dump

landslide A large amount of soil, rock, and land that moves down a slope

lava Rock in the form of a liquid that erupts from a volcano

magma Molten rock below Earth's surface

mines Places where rocks or minerals are extracted

non-renewable A material or resource that will run out

nutrients Chemicals that living things need to grow and stay healthy

ores Rocks that contain metal

pollutes Adds harmful substances to an environment

processed When a material is cleaned and changed to get it ready to be used

silicon An element used to make glass and computers

Stone Age A time from 2.5 million years ago to 11,000 years ago

turbines Devices with blades that spin around when a gas or liquid flows past them

volcanoes Landforms from which lava flows

Find out More

Books

Lawrence, Ellen. *What is the Rock Cycle?* (Rock-ology). Bearport Publishing, 2014.

Petersen, Christine. *Examine Minerals* (Geology Rocks!). Checkerboard Library, 2019.

Tomececk, Steve. *Ultimate Rockopedia: The Most Complete Rocks & Minerals Reference Ever*. National Geographic Children's Books, 2020.

Websites

www.dkfindout.com/us/earth/rocks-and-minerals
Read about rocks and take an interactive quiz.

www.mineralseducationcoalition.org
See pictures and activities about minerals, and find out how they are mined and how we use them.

www.nps.gov/subjects/geology/rocks-and-minerals.htm
Watch this National Parks Service video to find out how to identify the three different types of rocks.

www.youtube.com/watch?v=V21hFmZP5zM
This National Geographic video explores Earth's first rocks.

Index

Quiz answers
1. b; 2. b; 3. a; 4. a; 5. b